HIDE AND SEEK

HOW GOD IS HIDDEN BEHIND THE IMPENETRABLE CLOUD OF RELIGION

BY JAMES (PAT) PUGH

Hide and Seek
How God is hidden behind the impenetrable cloud of religion
by James (Pat) Pugh

Printed in the United States of America

ISBN 9781628398229

www.xulonpress.com

SPECIAL THANKS AND APPRECIATION TO:

- My wife, best friend, and my eternal love Carla

- My three boys, Jalin, Dominic, and James III. I love being your dad.

- My parents, James E., Senior, and Barbara Pugh. I could not have asked for a better dad and mom than you.

- My brothers and sisters, Michelle, Kelvin, Adrienne, Brian, and Dwayne. I love you guys. To ll of my nephews and nieces, I love you, too.

- The many other family and friends who pray for me, my family, and the ministry God called us to.

Thank you!

TABLE OF CONTENTS

PROLOGUE

I remember summers growing up as a kid in the Midwest where the days seemed as if they were 48 instead of 24 hours. We used to play *hide and seek* as the sun began to set. That gentle Midwest breeze would cool us off. I remember several kids on my street putting a foot into a circle and the leader saying "Eeny, meeny, miny, mo, catch a tiger by the toe, if he hollers let him go, eeny, meeny, miny, mo." Whoever's foot was left at the end had to stand, face forward, eyes closed against the telephone pole and begin to count 1,2,3,4.... all the way to 20. A mad dash began as 10-15 boys and girls began to look for the perfect hiding place before the counter got to 20. Kids would hide beneath cars, behind houses, behind bushes, in trees, or even somewhere in an open garage. Then the seeking began. After counting to 20, the seeker shouted a warning: "Ready or not, here I come," and began frantically trying to find those kids who hid in all kinds of places on our street. As soon as the seeker found someone hiding, he or she yelled, "Gotcha"!

I'm sure many of you remember playing this game for hours and all the childhood memories it brings back. Little did I know this game would describe my relationship with God for most of my life.

In Genesis 3, when man decided he wanted to govern himself instead of live under God's kingdom rule his initial reaction, once exposed, was to hide. "Then the man and his wife heard the sound of the Lord God as he was walking in the garden in the cool of the day, and they hid from the Lord God among the trees of the garden." Adam and Eve thought they had the perfect hiding place, and they believed if they found a tree large enough they could hide from the presence of God as He walked in the garden in the cool of the day. They fell for Satan's lie.

"For God knows that when you eat of it your eyes will be opened, and you will be like God, knowing good and evil." First of all, they were already like God. "Then God said, 'Let us make man in our image, in our likeness, and let them rule over the fish of the sea and the birds of the air, over the livestock, over all the earth, and over all the creatures that move along the ground'" (Genesis 1:26.) The fact that they thought they could hide from God proves the enemy's lie worked. In their minds, God had been reduced to the same level as the creature He created instead of the creator God.

They didn't realize it was not a game. God wasn't playing "hide and seek." Adam and Eve could not hide from God no matter where they went in the garden. They both were naked and exposed. For the first time they experienced shame and guilt. We are thankful God still pursues man as He did Adam and Eve in the garden. Not only did He find them, but "the Lord God made garments of skin for Adam and his wife and clothed them",(Genesis 3:21.) Once their sin was brought to light because God is love, He shed the blood of an animal and covered Adam and Eve with the skin. This act was a foreshadowing of the necessity of blood to cover man's sin. "In fact, the law requires that nearly everything be cleansed with blood, and without the shedding of blood there is no forgiveness" (Hebrews 9:22.) This act in Genesis was a precursor of what would be seen through the priesthood, temple worship, the kings and prophets, and eventually through the permanent sacrifice of Jesus.

"How much more, then, will the blood of Christ, who through the eternal Spirit offered himself unblemished to God, cleanse our consciences from acts that lead to death, so that we may serve the living God!"(Hebrews 9:14.) We are blessed to be in relationship with a God who loves us so much that He would pursue us. If it were up to us to pursue God, how many of us would still be hiding in the trees behind our guilt and shame as Adam and Eve did? I spent most of my life attempting to pursue God through religious activities instead of having God pursue me and cover my guilt and shame. I played "hide and seek" with God, but in my story God was hidden from me behind an impenetrable cloud called "religion," and no matter how many religious activities I participated in I was never able to find Him until I discovered His love and pursuit of me.

Chapter One

READY OR NOT, HERE I COME!

August 31, 1986, was a typical Sunday morning service at the church where I grew up. We had followed our routine. First a fast song, then a medium song, then a slow song, a prayer, scripture reading, and a fourth song. After the singing of this particular song, usually a slow song focusing on Jesus' death, we took communion.

After communion, the person leading our thoughts would say, "Now separate and apart from the communion we will take an offering. We would sing another song, usually a fast one to get the preacher excited to deliver the sermon. Yes, our worship service was scripted and very well organized—every *t* crossed and every *i* dotted to make sure our worship was decent, in order, and pleasing in God's sight. Now the sermon that morning was preached by my dad who was not a full-time (paid) preacher, but he filled in whenever the church was between preachers. I can't tell you what my dad preached about that Sunday, but what I do remember is his saying "if anyone wants Christ to be Savior and Lord of their life and put him on in baptism come forward as we sing the invitation song." Now I can't tell you the invitation song on that particular Sunday. Maybe it was "Why Not Tonight?" even though it was only 11:25 a.m., or maybe it was, "Just As I Am." Anyway, as the whole church stood up and began singing something was telling me to go forward and confess Jesus as Savior and Lord. Was this the day that I answered the call "Today, if you hear his voice, do not harden your hearts as you did in the rebellion" (Hebrews 3:15.)

I was seated four spaces from the aisle, so in order to get to the aisle I had to walk over a few people, but I didn't care. I finally made up my mind. I looked at the person next to me and quietly said, "Excuse me." I made my way past the four people and eventually to the aisle. My palms were sweaty; my throat had a lump like a softball in it.

I felt like I was walking the Green Mile, like I was on my way to the death chamber.(I realized years later that I actually was.) I made it to the front pew, sat down. My dad looked at me and said, "Do you have to go the bathroom?" My parents were from the old school, so we couldn't just get up and go to the bathroom without asking permission. My dad thought I took the death walk just to ask to go relieve myself.

I looked at my dad and told him, "I want to be baptized." In our church, when a person came forward they had to fill out a little blue card and put a check mark by the item they were requesting. The items included: prayers of the church for a particular situation, confessing of a sin, placing membership (remember this word *membership*), a request for a Bible study, or baptism. I checked the open box marked "I want to be baptized."

One of the elders of the church addressed the congregation and told them what I came forward to do. He then asked me before everyone if I believed that Jesus was the Christ, the Son of the living God. I felt a little like Peter when Jesus took the disciples to Caesarea Philippi and asked Peter, "Who do you say I am?" (Matthew 16:15.)

With the softball-sized lump in my throat, I answered, "Yes, I believe Jesus is the Christ, the son of the living God."

The elder took me upstairs to a changing room and I put on a white robe. While changing into the robe, I couldn't believe that I conjured up the nerves, walked up the middle aisle in front of 350 people, and made a public confession of Jesus Christ. That was totally out of my personality, so I knew it had to be the Holy Spirit calling me. As I walked down the steps of the baptistery and put one foot in the water I noticed how warm it was. A heater kept the water warm. I couldn't believe this was actually happening to me. I witnessed my two older siblings and several of my friends who had already made the decision to get baptized go through the same thing and probably feel the same butterflies in their stomachs that I was feeling at the time.

The elder helped me into the water, which came up to about my waist, and he said a few words. Then I remember his saying, "I now baptize you in the name of the Father, the Son, and the Holy Spirit." He took a handkerchief and covered my nose and my mouth, and next thing I remember is being dunked into the water. Or to use a more appropriate term, immersed. I remember coming up out of that water and feeling as light as a feather. I felt like I had really found God. I felt like the kid counting to twenty and then pursuing and seeking the ones who were hiding. I felt like I had found God. I felt like those few times I lied to my parents about beating up my little brother, those cookies I had stolen from Kroger, or those lustful thoughts I had as a 14-year-old teenage boy were all washed away. After I came down from the changing room with my church clothes back on, others who had already been baptized and became members greeted me and made statements like, "Congratulations," "Welcome to the family," and "I'm so proud of you." This made me feel special, but the best part was yet to come.

Chapter Two

MEMBERSHIP PRIVILEGES

I n my denomination, only those who had become members by being baptized were eligible to participate in the corporate worship service. Corporate worship can be defined as a local group of believers assembling to worship collectively. These meetings usually take place at designated times. Many Christians believe that according to their hermeneutic Sunday, the first day of the week, is the appropriate time for corporate worship.

For years I watched as my older brother and some of my male friends who had already taken the plunge get to pass out the communion trays, pray publicly, lead songs, and read Bible scriptures up front, elevated on the pulpit in front of everybody. It was almost like having a membership in a gym or at a prestigious golf course. You could enjoy all the amenities the club had to offer as long as you paid your membership dues. I wasn't an official member prior to my deciding to get baptized. I was on the outskirts looking at all my friends enjoy their membership privileges. The day I got baptized was special to me because until then I was not in the club. Once I came up out of the watery grave of baptism I was an official member of my local church. I had been on a trial membership. On being baptized I was upgraded to full membership, with Gold Status ready to start earning reward points.

Now I was officially eligible to serve on the communion table with my other friends who had already been baptized and had their Gold Status membership privileges. I could publicly do scripture reading or say a prayer. I was even now qualified to give the Wednesday evening devotion before we all broke away to our Bible classes. It was interesting to me that besides feeling light as a feather and having a few of my immoral habits forgiven,it didn't seem that much really changed in my life. Now that I was an official member I could exercise my Gold Status rewards privileges publicly. It was a great feeling. I was in the family now, and I had all the rights and privileges that other members had. I thought I had found what I was looking for. I felt like the kid who was seeking in *hide and seek* and now I found the last person. I'm no longer it. I don't have to seek anymore. God, I gotcha. Prior to August 31, 1986, I lived a pretty conservative life and that was not a bad thing. I had both of my parents at home who loved me and my siblings, worked very hard, and who made church, God, and spirituality the center of our family life. We would have family devotional evenings at our house. I had two sisters and three brothers, so there were eight of us all together. We lived on a *cul de sac* and used it to play baseball, football, or whatever other sports we could think of.

We had one particular evening during the week that was family devotional night. If a good football game was going on and we saw Daddy come to the door, we knew it was time to come in for family devotional, no matter what the score was of that particular game. We faithfully attended church gatherings and any other extracurricular activities the church offered besides Sunday morning, Sunday evening, and Wednesday evening service.

As a kid, I mostly despised our Sunday evening gatherings because at 5:30 p.m. we would have to leave for services that began at 6:00 p.m., and I never got to see the second half of the late NFL games during football season. This made me look like a square on the bus the next morning when I was asked if I saw the end of the San Francisco 49ers versus the Dallas Cowboys game.

In my denomination, during our gatherings we were taught there were five acts of proper worship and they were singing, praying, communion, collection, and preaching. Whenever the church gathered together for worship, in order for the worship to be acceptable these five acts had to take place. There are several key biblical scriptures that my religious denomination used to support their position on the five acts of worship.

The first and probably most important one is "On the first day of the week we came together to break bread. Paul spoke to the people and, because he intended to leave the next day, kept on talking until midnight" (Acts 20:7.) This verse is the support for why we meet on Sunday, why there is preaching every Sunday, and why we take communion every Sunday. This particular text is interpreted as the explanation for two of the five acts communion and preaching. Three other worship acts are also believed to be supported by New Testament scripture Let's take a look at them. "Now about the collection for God's people: Do what I told the Galatian churches to do. On the first day of every week, each one of you set aside a sum of money in keeping with his income, saving it up, so that when I come no collections will have to be made"(I Corinthians 16:1-2.)

The fourth act of worship would be singing—not just singing, but *a cappella* singing, which is singing without the accompaniment of an instrument. The two verses that are used to support this view are "Speak to one another with psalms, hymns and spiritual songs. Sing and make music in your heart to the Lord" (Ephesians 5:19.) "Let the word of Christ dwell in you richly as you teach and admonish one another with all wisdom, and as you sing psalms, hymns and spiritual songs with gratitude in your hearts to God" (Colossians 3:16.)

The fifth and final piece of the five acts of worship is prayer. One of many verses that support this idea is "They devoted themselves to the apostles' teaching and to the fellowship, to the breaking of bread and to prayer" (Acts 2:42.) I was taught that these five acts need to be actively present or the worship would not be in spirit and in truth (see John 4:24).

I mentioned how I despised Sunday evening worship, but not only did I despise it, I was totally confused by it. The purpose for Sunday night service confused me as a boy because when we went back for evening service I only participated in three of the five worship acts. We would sing together, pray together, and listen to the sermon together on Sunday evenings, but the communion and collection was only for those who were not there on Sunday morning. I guess on Sunday night it was okay to worship God with three out of the five worship acts for those of us who were there on Sunday morning. Although I suspect if I wanted to put a few extra dollars in the plate on Sunday evening nobody would have taken exception to that.

I also went to church camp almost every summer. As previously mentioned, we had a big family, so in order for us to participate in extracurricular activities we had to get scholarships from the church; my parents could not afford to send six kids to church camp every summer. We also attended some local and regional youth rallies and went to all the Vacation Bible Schools. So when I was baptized August 31, 1986, I already had a foundation of all these religious activities and events. I could already quote all the books of the Bible in order. I was pretty good already at scripture memorization. I lived a decent moral life with the exception

19

of some stolen cookies, an occasional lustful thought, and fighting with my brothers.

As a matter of fact I knew all the hand and body motions to the popular camp song "Father Abraham." I was secure in who I thought I was becoming, so my baptism was the only thing left to do in order to activate my membership and allow me to exercise my rights as a member of our local church. And that I did.

I didn't waste a lot of time using my membership rewards benefits at our local church. As a matter of fact, the very next Sunday after your baptism you were allowed to start serving in the corporate worship service. Now at my church when you were on call to serve in the worship, you would get your name written in the Sunday bulletin. For example, if I was leading a prayer or reading scripture my name appeared in print in the bulletin. How cool is that for a 14-year-old boy to headline his church's Sunday morning bulletin?

I led singing. or for a more contemporary term, worship leading. I did public prayers and led Wednesday night devotions. Our Wednesday evening devotions were at 7:00 p.m. We gathered together to sing one song and then an active member would give a devotional thought. After the devotional thought, an invitation, or altar call, to request prayers or accept Christ was given.

After the invitation we would all go to separate Bible classes. For example, the teenagers would attend one class, the young adults a class, and the junior high kids another class.

Shortly after my baptism, I was called on to lead the devotional thoughts for the evening and offer the invitation. I remember the days leading up to the Wednesday when I knew I had to lead the devotion and offer the invitation. I prepared like it was a Billy Graham crusade and I would be speaking in front of thousands. That Wednesday there were probably about 30-40 people in the audience as I debuted publicly preaching at church. I used the text "You are the light of the world. A city on a hill cannot be hidden" (Matthew 5:14.)

I probably spoke for no more than three minutes. The people who listen to me preach today are probably wondering what happened to those good old days. I thought the other members were proud of me for my decision to get baptized, but once I awed them with my mini-sermon that Wednesday I earned extra membership reward points. Other members again came up to me and told me how proud they were of me and that I would be a preacher like my daddy one day.

Now I was in awe of the membership rewards program. I didn't know that becoming a member would lead to other people's approval of me. This finding God thing was even more than I expected it to be. Out of all the wonderful compliments and acknowledgements from other members I always wondered why my parents never bought into this. They never praised us for passing out the communion trays, reading scripture, praying publicly, or leading singing. I always wondered in the back of my mind

Are they just not as easily impressed because I'm their son? Maybe it's because they see the real me at home. I figured out why my parents didn't fall into this game and I will explain later.

At our church, my family would have been like the Huxtables from the Cosby show. Now dad wasn't a doctor and mom wasn't a lawyer, but our family was very well respected. I honestly think people looked at us as the model black family at the church. Expectations for us were high because everyone in the church loved and respected my parents. My father preached for a whole year at the church while they were looking for a preacher and didn't take any money for it. He would travel around with his singing group and never took money for singing at a church program even if they offered it to him. My dad believed that he was just doing what he was supposed to do and for that he wasn't looking for any reward from a man. He wasn't looking for any pay, any credit, or any accolades. He was just living. This is why my parents didn't get caught up in the game of making us feel like we were something special for doing something that we were simply supposed to do. The very same people who put you up on a pedestal sometimes will be the same people who will watch you eventually fall. They will wonder when you fall *What happened to him? He used to be a good kid.*

On Sunday mornings my brothers and I would have on our Sunday best and line up at the communion table to hand out the communion trays.

Other members were even complimentary on the way we handed out the trays and how good we looked doing it. Other members would tell us how proud they were of us for the way we handed out the trays with the juice and crackers in it. This was awesome! Finding God was the best thing that had ever happened to me. People recognized things about me that I didn't even know were there. My identity was being shaped by what other reward members thought about my public image. I never realized how proud I could make other members by passing out trays, reading scripture, and leading songs. It was just too easy earning these reward points.

I had a routine every night before I went to bed. I would make sure I read three chapters out of the Bible and pray. Most nights I would be reading while falling into a deep coma-like sleep. I would fight through and finish because I had found God, and in order to stay in good standing I had to read the word daily. After I read those three chapters I prayed before I dozed off. I can remember being so sleepy that I would start the prayer on Monday night and finish it Tuesday morning once I woke up. I was operating out of pure obligation and duty. I spent all of junior high and high school accumulating membership rewards points at my local church.

My dad grew up singing in Alabama in his early life in the Baptist church and boy! could my daddy sing. He started a choir named *The Christian Jubilee*, and they traveled all over the Mid-west and the South singing at different church programs and functions. We would travel with

23

them most of the time, so we grew up hearing all of the popular *a cappella* music of the late '70s, '80s and '90s.

Since Daddy had a singing group, of course his kids had to follow suit, so we started singing in a group and named it *Victory*. The group was made up of some of our close friends who could sing. We merged with *The Christin Jubilee*, so whenever the singers would go somewhere and sing, *Victory* would be the opening act. We were developing a name and identity for ourselves locally and regionally. We had our own unique style different from *The Christian Jubilee*. The *Jubilees* had the old time gospel feel, and we were trying for a more modern style.

Now I thought local membership rewards program was good at my church, but little did I know the membership was good in other cities and with other local and regional churches.. After the *Jubilees* and *Victory* finished a program, members from other in other cities would tell us how much they loved our singing. I sang bass with *Victory* and the *Jubilees*, and let me tell you this: there is nothing like a good bass in *a cappella* singing. With *Victory* I could sing bass and make beats with my mouth. You see, my denomination believed that playing an instrument was not authorized by God. Since we couldn't play the drum, we would make up beats like a drum. Earlier, when I explained the five acts of worship, I referenced two verses that supported singing. Ephesians 5:19 and Colossians 3:16 both mention singing, and since there is no evidence for instruments, my denomination believed adding an instrument would be adding to the word of God. Both verses referenced making music in your heart and singing with gratitude in your heart. My denomination interpreted this verse to mean adding to God's word was sin. "I warn everyone who hears the words of the prophecy of this book: If anyone adds anything to them, God will add to him the plagues described in this book. And if anyone takes words away from this book of prophecy, God will take away from him his share in the tree of life and in the holy city, which are described in this book"(Revelation 22:18-19.)

Adding instruments was a direct violation of scripture and was considered a salvation issue. So when I found God in 1986, I wanted to make sure that I did everything to keep Him, and not jeopardize my membership rewards. If they said no instruments then that is what we did. Again, because we couldn't actually play an instrument we would make beats with our mouths to sound like an instrument because we were told the Bible says singing was to come from our hearts and not an instrument. It was like gospel music merging with the "Fat Boys" or "Doug E Fresh." (You old school "hip hop fans get it.) So we could sound like a drum but our denomination would not allow us to play one.

This making beats with our mouth would drive the crowd wild. People would get up on their feet when they heard that bass sound dropping. The harmonies in the background and my baby brother singing lead on the old "*Straight Company* song "Something about King Jesus" Was a show-stopper.-

Now finding God led me to another talent, and people really responded to this much more than the passing out of Lord's Supper trays and doing scripture reading. I sang with the groups up until the time I went to college. I was a teenage boy singing in these two groups with people giving us all kinds of attention, especially the young ladies. Meeting a young lady at church had a simple solution, become a part of a singing group who could really sing and half the battle of meeting the ladies is done. At 16 and 17-years-old, this finding God along with membership rewards was the best thing ever. As mentioned before, when I was baptized one of the moral issues that was washed away was lust. My history with lust became problematic for me when we would go out of town to sing. So many nice-looking young ladies watched us perform on stage. Instead of giving God glory and praising Him for who He is I would be looking out into the crowd to see who I wanted to approach after the singing program was over. I had a handle on the instrumental music part, but I totally ignored Jesus' "But I tell you that anyone who looks at a woman lustfully has already committed adultery with her in his heart" (Matthew 5:28.)

Here I was, more concerned with singing the right notes and keeping the pace of the song while I lustfully looked into the crowd to locate attractive young ladies. It is amazing that a person could be on a stage singing about a God and have a heart so far from Him. "The Lord says: "These people come near to me with their mouth and honor me with their lips, but their hearts are far from me. Their worship of me is made up only of rules taught by men" (Jeremiah 29:13.)

Chapter Three

THE FOOLISH MAN BUILT HIS HOUSE UPON THE SAND

I remember in Vacation Bible School I learned a song they taught us named "The Wise Man Built His House Upon a Rock." A verse in that song goes like this:

"The foolish man built his house upon the sand,

the foolish man built his house upon the sand,

the foolish man built his house upon the sand,

and the rain came tumbling down.

Oh, the rain came down and the floods came up,

the rain came down and the floods came up,

the rains came down and the floods came up

and the house on the sand went SPLAT!."

Now I knew that this cute little VBS song was not talking about me because my house was built on the rock Jesus Christ—or so I thought. I had confessed him as Savior. I was baptized into Christ and I went to church camp every summer. I sang with two *a cappella* groups and my membership reward points were steadily stacking up. Remember I found God so I was secure in what everybody told me about myself.

I did have a social life outside of our fellowship growing up. I attended Colerain Senior High School and had some really good friends there. I was also a decent basketball player. The only dreams I really had of college were playing basketball one day in Lexington, Kentucky, Tobacco Road, or on the campus of Georgetown University.

Then reality set in. My senior year came, but letters did not. Nobody was even interested in me. My grades were average, but I thought at least a Division II school or junior college would give me a chance. To make a long story short, I sent some game tapes of a few of my high school games to a small Christian school in West Virginia affiliated with our denomination. My cousin was about to attend there that fall and the coach told me I could come and walk on. At the time, the school was competing in the National Small Collegiate Athletic Association (NSCAA). I didn't care what they called it, I just wanted to play ball. At the time of my high school graduation I was working in a shoe store in the mall and had no further plans for my future. College wasn't really something that was pushed or encouraged in our house. My parents didn't go to college although they wanted to, so it was not something they really pushed on us. When I graduated from high school I hadn't taken the ACT or SAT. I hadn't filled out one college application. I thought I would just find a job or keep the one at the shoe store and work my way up to management.

That August, after graduation, I ended up packing my belongings and heading off to that small Christian college. It was a small campus with only a few black people. Growing up I always lived in all black communities, so my worldview was shaped by where I lived. In West Virginia, my worldview was challenged and I felt culture shock, living in a dormitory with only a few blacks. Again, this college was affiliated with our religious denomination, and I wondered why so few blacks represented the total enrollment of a denomination that was claiming to be the one true church. Of the few blacks that were on campus, the majority were the athletes, so I naturally associated myself with them and withdrew from everyone else. These athletes were labeled as the heathens, the unbelievers, and the ones who lived wildly and recklessly.

My parents dropped me off on Saturday and made the four- hour drive back to Cincinnati. I remember other kids having bank accounts set up for them to begin their venture in college. My dad handed me a $20 bill, gave me a hug, and drove off. I spent that $20 that evening going to the movies with some guys from the basketball team. I pretended that I had money because I had gotten pretty good at pretending at church all those years. So there I was. Classes hadn't even started yet and I was not only miserable on this campus with no black people but I was broke. I called my parents that night and pleaded with them to come and get me. I was not staying at a school in the hills of West Virginia with only a few black athletes on campus. Of course my parents were not about to come back and get me, so I just had to stick it out.

Remember—four years earlier I had found God, so surviving on a West Virginia Christian college campus with other reward members shouldn't be that hard, right?

As for many freshman starting their first venture away from home I felt excitement, anticipation, and a sense of freedom. There was no one there to tell me what to do, when to get up, when to go to class, who I could hang out with, and where I could go. Of course our school had rules because of the religious affiliation, but I still felt a huge sense of liberty being away from mom and Dad for the first time. What would I do with this newfound freedom? How would I exercise this liberty that I was experiencing for the first time in my life? My foundation was about to experience a real storm for the first time.

Let's just say my freshman year in college was one of the darkest periods of my life. I'm a young 18-year-old who found God or so I thought. Singing in church groups, attending church camps, VBS, youth rallies, passing out communion trays, leading singing, and praying in public. I get to college and totally forget who I am.

With this new-found liberty I began doing things that were totally out of character of who I was raised to be. I was in nightclubs on the weekends, drinking, at hotel parties, behaving inappropriately with women. Going out all night and not returning until early in the morning. Sneaking in and out of the dorms, breaking all the rules that the college had set up for us for our protection. Some of you reading this may be able to relate to what it is like to live under rules, laws, and structure all of your life, then to get away from your safety net and realize your foundation was never really as solid as you thought it was.

I realized that my problem was not that I went to college and forgot who I was. I went to college and never knew who I was to begin with. I was never able to self-discover through the Holy Spirit who I was as I grew up. I was too busy pretending to be somebody else in public while the real me was covered in the impenetrable cloud of religious activities. No one could convey to me who I was at this time or what my purpose was because I thought I had it figured out already, based on other people's perception of me. When I was outside of the church's influence, I was a basketball player. When I was around church people I was a bass singer for two spiritual singing groups, a guy who could lead singing, pray publicly, and lead Wednesday devotions.

During my freshman year in college, I was suspended from school right before Christmas break. I was constantly in the dean's office explaining why I couldn't make it back to the dorm before curfew, and I had an arrogant attitude. I believe that most of my behavioral issues stemmed from what I call an identity crisis. I did not know who I was and what my purpose for being alive was. It caused me to develop a huge chip on my shoulder. If I could give the chip on my shoulder a name I would have called it Rebellion.

Rules without relationship lead to rebellion. But I had found God, and I thought my foundation was solid like the wise man. One thing I realized quickly is that the wise builder was called wise for a reason. Wisdom is the application of knowledge. The wise man not only knew that he needed to build a strong foundation, but he acted on what he knew. He anticipated strong winds and high water prior to building a structure on his foundation. He took into consideration what he needed to do before he built a structure.

We sometimes neglect the most important aspect of building a solid life here on this earth, and attempt to build a structure on a shaky foundation. The foundation must be strong enough to hold the weight of whatever we are building. When engineers and contractors are ready to build a structure, whether a house, office building, or a stadium, more money and resources go into the foundation so the structure has a firm place to stand.

My freshman year of college I began to build a structure on the foundation that had been laid up to this point in my life. I had a structure built on gaining identity from other people by singing in groups, church camps, VBS, youth rallies, and membership points at church. This was my foundation. It looked good on the outside, but lacked what was needed to hold the weight of what I was carrying. The first time some real adversity blew against my structure the whole building collapsed and I was exposed.

Everything I thought I was and everything I thought I knew imploded right in front of me and everyone else. What I attempted to do in secret came out in the light as my structure came tumbling to the ground. Can you imagine how hard it was to go back and face the very same people that helped build this false you and put you high upon this pedestal for looking good passing out communion trays?

The most difficult phone call I ever made was to my parents to explain to them why I got suspended from a Christian college. Honestly, of all the people whose opinions mattered to me, none mattered more than my parents'.

I got a firsthand experience of what the prodigal son felt like when he ended up in the pig pen eating pigs' food. Before I called home that evening to break the news, just like the prodigal son I rehearsed a speech to lighten the impact of the news that I had been suspended. "The son said to him, 'Father, I have sinned against heaven and against you. I am no longer worthy to be called your son'" (Luke 15:21.) This is exactly how I felt. Had all the years of singing, passing out communion, church camps, and leading devotions led me to this point? I didn't feel worthy anymore. How could I look my parents and the other reward members in the face again?

The prodigal son requested something very interesting during this rehearsal speech he prepared to tell his dad. He wanted his father to demote him to a hired servant in the place of sonship. Do you see the problem with this? Many young people who grow up in a denomination like I did have this kind of identity crisis. They identify more with the denomination and working for righteousness rather than becoming the righteousness of Christ. The son wanted to be a hired servant because he thought if he worked hard enough he could earn some of the respect back he had lost from his father. We can't do enough good works to be saved, to make our heavenly Father like us more, or to win His approval. We don't get blessings from God because we work for them. God is the giver of all good things because that is who He is, not because we work for them. If the prodigal son fell from son ship, why would he ask his father to restore him to merely hired help? (Matthew 20:1-16) He did not fall from the status of hired help, so if true restoration is going to take place then he must be restored back to the position he fell from. I call the prodigal son's request "pigpen theology." I define it as viewing ourselves according to our circumstance instead of our position. Because of the son's current position he wanted to address his father out of his circumstance rather than his position. He no longer viewed himself as his Father viewed him, but viewed himself according to his current living condition. How many people have a tough time looking themselves in the mirror because they feel like they are a failure? They don't think God wants to be their Father anymore on account of bad behavior.

If we would stop worrying about how other people view us when we make mistakes and focus on how God sees us, we would come running back to him every time. "You are all sons of God through faith in Christ Jesus, for all of you who were baptized into Christ have clothed yourselves with Christ" (Galatians 3:26-27.) Paul uses the word "clothed" in this text.

Clothes play a huge part in shaping the identity of people. We wear certain brand names of clothes and shoes because it makes a statement about our status and how we want other people to view us. We wear brand names of top designers to identify with them because we are not sure about our own identity. It amazes me how people will promote and advertise a specific brand name but never get compensated for it, or refer to their favorite sports team as "we" and put on the jerseys and hats of their favorite player. People are looking for something to identify with in order to feel accepted and be a part of something that is bigger than they are.

Paul tells us that we ought to wear Christ or clothe ourselves with Christ and our identity would never be in question about who and whose we are because we are declared as sons of the Father.

So many young people growing up in denominations fail to understand their initial position. My concern was that my membership reward points would begin to be deducted for bad behavior, when the real position I fell from was sonship. My parents handled my suspension so graciously and with so much mercy. They didn't put a robe on me, a ring on my finger, sandals on my feet, and kill a fattened calf, but they loved me through a very difficult time. I would say in their own way that my parents restored me in the same manner as the prodigal son's father restored him.

I wasn't sure if I was going to return to school after that eye opening first semester, but my dad said something to me that I have never forgotten. He told me to go back to school and make a difference. Sounds simple, but it is profound. My dad spoke a lot of kingdom language even though if you would have asked him he would not have known he was speaking kingdom language. In so many words he told me to go back to school and be yeast in dough, be a light in darkness, be the salt of the earth. He didn't mention anything about membership rewards points; he simply told me to take the kingdom to that school.

Now, my biggest dilemma was that my foundation was shaky at best. In order for me to take the kingdom to the school I would need to burn the prior foundation of public image and religious activities. I would need to rebuild one that could not be shaken.

At the conclusion of the sermon on the hill, Jesus said, "Therefore everyone who hears these words of mine and puts them into practice is like a wise man who built his house on the rock" (Matthew 7:24.) Even though I grew up in a denomination and heard plenty of sermons, I was like the people Isaiah prophesied about. He said, "Go and tell this people: 'Be ever hearing, but never understanding: be ever seeing, but never perceiving.' Make the heart of this people calloused; make their ears dull and close their eyes. Otherwise they might see with their eyes, hear with their ears, understand with their hearts, and turn and be healed" (Isaiah 6:9-10.) This prophesy described me down to the very core of my being. I was forever hearing, but not understanding. As long as I was gaining membership reward points nothing else mattered. As long as other people viewed me the way I thought they should everything was fine. In a sense I was a fraud, and there was nothing authentic about me or my walk with God. I had a relationship built on rules, regulations, laws, and keeping a good public image.

I decided to go back to school and I finished my freshman year with my faith shaken. It is obvious that faith is something that can be passed down and can be a part of our family heritage. As a matter of fact, what better inheritance can we leave for our children and the generations to follow than a legacy of faith?

I am reminded of the heritage of faith of young Timothy as Paul recalls it. "I have been reminded of your sincere faith, which first lived in your grandmother Lois and in your mother Eunice and, I am persuaded, now lives in you also" (II Timothy 1:5.)

I had two great examples in my life of people who walked by faith and not by sight. I watched as my parents did everything they could to keep our family together, keep their marriage solid, and above all keep God first in everything we did. We can't deny the power of God in our family because my parents always acknowledged Him and taught us about Him. My parents were so good at this that we grew up poor but didn't really realize we were poor. My parents never abused us or treated us harshly, always had smiles on their face, and were some of the most hospitable people you would ever meet.

Our house was always full of life, joy, peace, and people. Although we didn't have much materially, people were always at our house. We lived in a tiny house with three small bedrooms the size of some people's walk-in closets today. For some reason, our house was always full. My parents were people of faith and lived a life of love and faith in Christ Jesus. I sincerely believe that no matter how much faith your parents or grandparents have, it does not become yours until you understand it for yourself. I had great parental role models who did the best they could to teach us how to live by faith, but my faith didn't start to develop until my sophomore year of college when I was nineteen.

After a horrible first year in college, I went back with a different attitude and a new perspective. I can remember early in the fall of 1992 while in my dorm I prayed to God and told him that I was going to read the Bible for transformation instead of simple information. I told God that I wanted to forget everything I was ever taught and I wanted Him to teach me. I told God I wanted to believe in Him because I'm convinced that He is real and not because someone else told me. I wanted to have a faith that could move a mountain.

When we ask God specifically, I believe He gives us specific answers. I begin to literally rip through the pages of the Bible like a crazy man. I couldn't get enough and I was coming back for more. I started listening to the text and asking the Spirit to interpret what certain things meant. For the first time in my life, I allowed the Word to tell me what it was saying instead of my reading it and telling it what it says.

I requested from God that I wanted to have faith to move mountains and the first mountain that needed to be moved was the shaky foundation of religious activity. I can remember discovering things in the Word of God that didn't necessarily line up with what my denomination taught. I had to make a decision.

Do I believe the Word of God or a denominational creed? I would discover a biblical truth and call home and question my parents about what we were taught in our denomination. They would ask me, "What are they teaching you at that school?" The thing is, it was not the school teaching me these things—it was the Holy Spirit. The school where I was affiliated with our denomination, so they held firm to the creeds and doctrines more so than my parents did. I was seeing God work through His Word and the Holy Spirit in a way I had never experienced before. This was the process of discovering through the Word my true identity as a son of God.

I began growing in the grace and knowledge of our Lord and Savior Jesus Christ by leaps and bound. Early my sophomore year, not only did God show Himself to me, but He made good on a promise in his Word. "Delight yourself in the Lord and he will give you the desires of your heart" (Psalm 37:4.) For the first time in my life it was a delight to pursue and seek after God and not a duty. I was on a chase after Him and I had tunnel vision. This particular promise in Psalm said if our delight is in the Lord then He will give our hearts' desire.

I can remember the first day I saw her. I was walking up the hill with my roommate and she was walking down the hill with her volleyball teammates. Her name was Carla Oliveira. She was from the east coast— Attleboro, Massachusetts. We fell in love within a few months of meeting and have been happily married for more than 18 years. When Carla and I met, I was a sophomore and she was a freshman. She came to the Christian college because she was at a point in her life also where she wanted her faith to be her own. She had always had a heart for God, but like a lot of teenagers lived on the fence of trusting God completely and flirting with the world.

When God led us to each other, the pursuit became a dual mission. We both wanted the same thing—an authentic relationship with God. We would sit at the picnic tables under the trees with our Bibles open, reading and wrestling with the scriptures. I can recall some of our conversations being so intense that some of Carla's friends would walk by and think we were arguing and on the verge of breaking up. We were so serious about pursuing God that we didn't care what it looked like to other people. We just knew we wanted God.

This pursuit of God got so intense that two of my roommates and I stopped going to the local church's Wednesday evening Bible classes because it was just not enough for us anymore. We had moved past the elementary teachings and desired some solid food that would help us grow. The local churches would shuttle vans to campus and pick up students who attended their Wednesday Bible class. We would wait until all the shuttles ran and use a hanger to break into one of the lecture halls every Wednesday. It started out with just three of us. We continued to do our secret Wednesday meetings that whole year until word start getting around campus.

Before we knew it our secret Bible study was leaked and a few more people wanted to attend. Attendance on the shuttle buses began to decrease slowly and more people began to attend this not so secret Bible study. This Wednesday Bible study became the talk of campus, and before we knew it there were 75 people packed in this lecture hall. A lot of the athletes who had no church background would attend. People from denominations besides ours would attend, and it was 100% Holy Spirit led. The worship was awesome, the bible studies challenging, and people were being saved, delivered, and set free. This meeting was free from denomination creeds, rules, and laws. It was 70-80 college kids who were seeking the Lord, praying together, and loving each other as citizens of the kingdom are supposed to do.

What was God up to in my life? I had never experienced God in this way before. It was different. It wasn't religion, it wasn't a bunch of do's and don'ts. It wasn't about keeping up a public image. God had shown himself to be real in my life. He was speaking to me loud and clear through the revelation of His Word. I had been baptized in 1986, but it wasn't until seven years later that true transformation began right before my eyes. A spiritual metamorphosis was taking place as God slowly began to show Himself and pursue me.

Chapter Four

THE B.I.B.L.E.

W hen I was really young growing up, we used to sing another children's song called "The B.I.B.L.E." It goes something like this:

The B.I.B.L.E

now that's the book for me.

I stand alone on the word of God

the B.I.B.L.E.

At the end we would all shout "BIBLE!"

II Timothy 3:16 supports the Bible as being the inspired Word of God. Psalms 119:106 describes the word as a lamp unto my feet and the light unto my path. Hebrews 4:12 claims it is "living and active sharper than any double-edged sword." I grew up with what I view as a healthy reverence for the inspired Word of God. The first thing I can remember about the Bible is memorizing the books in order. The next thing I remember is reading and memorizing the narratives: Creation, Adam and Eve, Cain and Abel, Moses and the Exodus, Samson and Delilah, he birth of Christ, and Paul's missionary journeys. These stories fascinated me as a kid and the characters in these stories were some of my heroes growing up.

Even as a young child I believe God gave me enough faith to believe what I was reading. When the Bible would say something like "Never will I leave you; never will I forsake you" Hebrews 13:5), I believed it with all my heart. Now I knew the characters in the Bible stories lived long ago, so one way I could make the Bible relevant to my life as a kid was to watch how other reward members believed it. When you are young there are things that happen and because of your lack of understanding they go right by you. As you get older and begin to understand a little better then you become more vulnerable to what you see.

Our local church in my denomination was very diverse, and I don't just mean racially. In our denomination our church was the only racially diverse church in the city. We were socio-economically diverse. (Our family made up the percentage of poor.) We had elderly people, middle aged, professionals, college students, junior high/high school age, single families, and families with small children.

My perspective of who God was and what He could do was first based upon how I saw God in my parents, then how other reward members lived based on what they believed about God. I understand we live in a fallen world, but children tend to trust and believe the best about everyone. We think that if the God of all these cute Sunday school songs is everything to you then he ought to be everything to other reward members who sing and pray to Him also.

In my early childhood, as far as I can remember, this held to be true. I remember the songs we learned, memorization of scripture, church camp, VBS, and singing with the groups. Life was good. Then all of a sudden, reward members whom I looked up to, spent time with, and loved began to divorce and separate. As I got a little older, one of the ministers of our denomination left his wife and kids and ran off with another woman. The songs, youth trips, church camps, and all the memorizing of scripture began to lose significance to me. Suddenly babies were being born out of wedlock, families were getting divorced, and attendance at the local church began to shrink. People transferred their membership rewards to other local churches because they didn't like the policies any longer. They were able to receive better benefits from other local churches with the same rewards program.

I heard sermons about evangelizing and having a heart for the lost while we drove right pass them three times a week. We were talking about how much we love them instead of doing anything about it. As a young kid my thoughts were, *Are we just talking about how awesome this God is? Singing about how great he is, traveling to different cities to sing about him to other reward members? Getting excited about the songs describing him while nothing changes around us?* It seems my denomination was more fascinated with the stories in the book than the one who inspired the book. Reward members are still splitting up, young girls are still getting pregnant before marriage, young boys in some of the local churches of our denomination are selling drugs and going to jail.

What happened to "I stand alone on the word of God the B.I.B.L.E?" By the time I got into high school, I was totally confused about the Bible. If this is the revealed Word of God, the power to save, then why is everyone leaving? I can recall one particular verse where Paul says "I am not ashamed of the gospel, because it is the power of God for the salvation of everyone who believes; first for the Jew, then for the Gentile" (Romans 1:16.) This Word, this gospel was to have a demonstration of power attached to it that would manifest itself in the lives of the people. Paul, when he addressed the church in Corinth, stated, "My message and my preaching were not with wise and persuasive words, but with a demonstration of the Spirit's power" (I Corinthians 2:4.)

The missing link was the Spirit's power accompanied by the preaching of the message. The Bible camps, VBS, youth trips, and all of my religious activities were not wrong. They just lacked the Spirit's power. Paul's message and preaching was backed up by power, and that power came from the Holy Spirit. This Holy Spirit power is what infuses the people who make up the church to obey and be the hands and feet of Jesus on earth.

My denomination had a quote that we lived by: *"Speak where the Bible speaks, and be silent where the Bible is silent."* This meant that whatever we did was according to written scripture, and the Bible gave us authority to do it. If the Bible is silent on a matter or it is not written, then we don't do it. This was the main defense for the instrumental music issue. My denomination believed the Bible gave no authority for instrumental music, and there was no evidence in the New Testament of saints using instruments. I said earlier in this chapter that by the time I was in high school I was totally confused about the Bible because the same Bible that gave no evidence for instrumental music gives evidence and authority for spiritual gifts. I never witnessed certain gifts being exercised among my denomination. The apostle Paul in his first letter to the church at Corinth says, "Now about spiritual gifts, brothers, I do not want you to be ignorant. You know that when you were pagans, somehow or other you were influenced and led astray to mute idols. Therefore I tell you that no one who is speaking by the Spirit of God says, 'Jesus be cursed,' and no one can say, 'Jesus is Lord,' except by the Holy Spirit. There are different kinds of gifts, but the same Spirit. There are different kinds of service, but the same Lord. There are different kinds of working, but the same God works all of them in all men. Now to each one the manifestation of the Spirit is given for the common good. To one there is given through the Spirit the message of wisdom, to another the message of knowledge by means of the same Spirit, to another faith by the same Spirit, to another gifts of healing by that one Spirit, to another miraculous powers, to another prophecy, to another distinguishing between spirits, to another speaking in different kinds of tongues, and to still another the interpretation of tongues. All these are the work of one and the same Spirit, and he gives them to each one, just as he determines" (I Corinthians 12:1-11.)

The Word declares that the Spirit gives gifts to members of the body that are manifested for the common good of the church. If we take a look again at the popular axiom "Speak where the Bible speaks, and be silent where the Bible is silent," the Bible is loud and clear about spiritual gifts. The reason I was so confused at this point about the Bible is because the instrumental music argument was based on scriptural silence and spiritual gifts was spoken loud and clear, but I never saw them exercised in my denomination. Is it possible to go to the scriptures like we would Golden Corral on a Sunday afternoon and simply pick the things that we like and leave everything else for someone else? This is how confusion infiltrates the body of Christ when what the Word of God plainly says is left up to the interpretation of a particular denomination.

This is why we see so much confusion among denominations about which one is the right one. We see the spirit of competition in the body of Christ as opposed to the spirit of unity. Denominations are concerned about which one is the fastest growing, which ones are declining. Ministers and pastors abuse their authority and participate in elicit affairs with members and misuse church funds, while still trying to follow the denomination's doctrinal creeds to a science. Jesus also warns about people like this "Woe to you, teachers of the law and Pharisees, you hypocrites! You clean the outside of the cup and dish, but inside they are full of greed and self-indulgence" (Matthew 23:25.)

I've often wondered why the most charismatic, energetic, extraverted personality, and effective communicator was put up in the pulpit. Now don't get me wrong. These traits are not bad to have. But what about characteristics such as integrity, character, and—most importantly—being full of the Holy Spirit? One trait that was a common denominator with servants of God during the early church was they were full of the Holy Spirit. "Brothers choose seven from among you who are known to be full of the Holy Spirit and wisdom" (Acts 6:3.) They chose Stephen, a man full of faith and of the Holy Spirit; also Phillip, Procorus, Nicanor, Timon, Parmenas, and Nicolas from Antioch, a convert to Judaism. They presented these men to the apostles, who prayed and laid their hands on them. In this context the church was experiencing growth and there was some complaining concerning the food distribution between the Grecian and Hebraic widows. The apostles delegated the work to seven men full of the Holy Spirit and faith.

I want to make a point here concerning the characteristics the 21st century church in my denomination use to appoint ministers compared to those of the first century church. Here are 3 real-life churches from my denomination, whose name I will leave out, that are searching for ministers to fill positions. Take a look at these qualifications and compare them to those in Acts. Now keep in mind these are different ministerial positions from the seven men in Acts, but the character of the ministers should be the same.

"Qualifications for a minister: Bachelors a must, Masters welcome, age 30-45, marital status required married. Position expectations: friendly, out going [sic], some humor, good speaker, and handsome." Yes, this is a real qualification from a university's website in my denomination. This particular church requires a handsome man who is funny.

Next position, a church in search of a youth minister: wants "someone who has prior youth experience, successful track record for youth group involvement and growth, college graduate with four year bachelor degree, good verbal communication skills, social network familiarity, good computer skills, strong organizational skills, creative presentation styles, willingness to work with potential involvement and establish youth committee, has a vision for youth ministry and will work diligently to implement the vision, has a heart of inclusion for all kids in the group no matter their level of previous involvement, and will be intentional and have a plan for building relationships."

Final position is for an Involvement Minister: This is a newly created position over the last several years. The Involvement minister will have many responsibilities. He will be the full time song leader, build programs for young families, promote parent led youth ministry, teach classes, and do occasional fill-in preaching for the pulpit minister.

The church puts qualified men in positions of leadership who have computer skills, personal communication skills, and the right education, but are these men filled with the Holy Ghost and wisdom? What if this person possesses the necessary qualities looked for by the elders and search committees, but lacks the anointing of the Holy Ghost? "But the Lord said to Samuel, "Do not consider his appearance or his height, for I have rejected him. The Lord does not look at the things man looks at. Man looks at the outward appearance, but the Lord looks at the heart"(I Samuel 16:7.) I often wonder *Would God appoint the same people we appoint in leadership today in the body of Christ?* "When they saw the courage of Peter and John and realized that they were unschooled, ordinary men, they were astonished and they took note that these men had been with Jesus" (Acts 4:13.)

Imagine for a moment applying for a ministry position in a church today. Under education you fill in unschooled. Under qualities you fill in ordinary. Would you have a chance of getting a ministry position in the 21st century church? Would you rather have someone leading the people of God who is a good communicator, has good computer skills, is familiar with social networking, and has at least a bachelor's degree, or have someone like Peter and John who have been hanging out with Jesus?

One thing we were encouraged not to do is question the authority of "the man of God," the preacher, because after all he went to school and received a quality education from what is called a brotherhood school—a school affiliated with a particular denomination or a preaching school with the same affiliation. Now I have some post undergraduate education, and it was a true blessing to be able to study in seminary. By no means am I under-valuing the significance of higher learning.

I can remember especially among the predominantly African American churches in my denomination how the ministers elevated themselves one to another. I call it "Pastor worship." During certain programs, the ministers would all come out together in their expensive suits, gold watches, gold rings, and gold bracelets. They would get a special table at the fellowship meals and eat off the good china while everyone else ate off paper plates and plastic spoons. They had their own parking space in the church building parking lot. I remember when the visiting minister would get up to preach and be introduced. The introduction would take five minutes, listing all of his degrees, accomplishments, and awards. The only thing that was missing was the limousine and the red carpet (although I have seen the limousine). It was like a celebrity, a movie star, a famous entertainer, or athlete was being introduced.

Jesus warned the crowd he was addressing about people like that: "They love the place of honor at banquets and the most important seats in the synagogues; they love to be greeted in the marketplaces and to have men call them 'Rabbi'" (Matthew 23:7.)

Do you remember reading in Matthew 5 the sermon on the hill? If you had to introduce Jesus before he got up to preach, what would you say? It would literally take an eternity to read all of his accomplishments, but before he preached there was no introduction. It simply says, "Now when he saw the crowds, he went up on a mountainside and sat down. His disciples came to him, and he began to teach them"(Matthew 5:1.) Wow! Jesus needs no introduction— just somewhere to sit, and then he begins the greatest sermon ever preached.

Also, Paul mentions all of his accomplishments, but then says, "But whatever was to my profit I now consider loss for the sake of Christ"(Philippians 4:7.) I suggest ministerial candidates go through their list of degrees and accomplishments to intimidate the listeners so they won't be questioned about anything they preach. Remember this: whoever controls the minds of the people controls the culture.

The Bible was supposed to be this liberating book that brought life to people, that brought truth, that brought light to darkness. It was supposed to be the book that brought man the revelation of the kingdom of God. I remember it as a book that was used to win religious arguments and prove our denomination was right and everyone else was wrong. The difference from what I learned growing up and what the Lord started showing me my sophomore year was like two people looking out the same window, looking at the same thing, but having two different perspectives on what was viewed.

Chapter Five

BELIEF OR BEHAVIOR

John 20:24-27: "Now Thomas (called Didymus), one of the Twelve, was not with the disciples when Jesus came. So the other disciples told him, "We have seen the Lord!" But he said to them, "Unless I see the nail marks in his hands and put my hand into his side, I will not believe it." A week later his disciples were in the house again, and Thomas was with them. Though the doors were locked, Jesus came and stood among them and said, "Peace be with you!" Then he said to Thomas, "Put your finger here; see my hands. Reach out your hand and put it into my side. Stop doubting and believe." (John 20:24-27.)

Thomas got the chance that so many of us could only dream of. To have all of his doubts answered about whether or not Jesus' claims as the risen Savior were true or not. Jesus invited Thomas to touch his hands where they drove the nails, and to touch his side where they pierced him with a spear. After this there would be no question in Thomas' mind whether or not Jesus is who he says he is. After Thomas was able to see and touch the tangible evidence, his reply was "My Lord and My God!" (John 20:28.) Would Thomas ever have another reason to doubt again? Would he ever again question Jesus' claim as Savior and Lord? After Thomas' experience with Jesus in that house, could his foundation ever be shaken again?

The more God shows us, the more responsible we are for what we witness. Once Jesus allowed Thomas to touch him, he told him to stop doubting and believe. After Jesus allowed Thomas to touch him, he said something profound. "Then Jesus told him, "Because you have seen me, you have believed; blessed are those who have not seen and yet have believed" (John 20:29.)

This is a grand slam statement, a 58-yard field goal with 00:00 left on the clock to win the game, or a 3-pointer at the buzzer down by 2! Jesus shifts the focus from Thomas who was right there with him to the thousands and millions of people who would never have the opportunity that Thomas had. Jesus speaks a blessing to those who wouldn't have the opportunity to touch him, but would have the faith as if they were in that house with Jesus and were able to touch him as Thomas did.

Let's revisit Jesus' words "stop doubting and believe" (John 20:27.) My denomination may have changed Jesus' statement to "stop doubting and behave." We put much emphasis on behavior and did everything possible to make sure our behavior was in line with the beliefs of our particular denomination. I can remember that the emphasis was more on our behavior when we were gathered together in the building going through religious activities than outside the building walls. We had to make sure that we did not behave like any other denominations because, after all, our claim was "we are patterned after the first church." My denomination took pride in believing that our heritage went back to AD 33. This is when it is believed the church started.

Therefore, our behavior needed to be in line with that of the behavioral pattern of the early church. As I got older I begin to see some inconsistencies in how we were trying to behave and how the early church behaved. All the songs with the cute hand motions, Bible camps, youth rallies, and religious gatherings, the passing of communion trays, singing in groups, leading songs, etc., really had nothing to do with how the first century Christians behaved. I mastered those things so well in my mind I thought I had the behavioral pattern expected of me down to an art. Then I read the book of Acts and it shocked me! The early church in Acts met with each other daily, ate together, witnessed wonders and miracles. And then this is really what shocked me: they would sell their possessions and goods and give to anyone as he had need. These ancient believers created a culture of the kingdom of heaven that was not merely based on performing five acts properly in worship. As far as my memory goes back, I can never recall anyone behaving like this. I never saw people healed, miraculous wonders, and people actually selling their possessions and then giving to those who needed from the proceeds of the sale.

I told you in chapter 2 that our family was included with the poor percentage of our local church growing up. My dad worked hard, but I remember a time in his life where in a period of four years he was without work and couldn't find a job. There were six kids in our family and my mom stayed at home to take care of the eight of us. Dad was the only breadwinner in the family. We were faithful attendees at our local church, so when my dad came upon tough times those four years, we just knew that the behavioral pattern of the local church would line up with that of the first century church because that is what our church took pride in and grounded themselves in. We knew there would be no questions about getting help from our local church, right?

Let's just say most of the people didn't even realize we were in such a struggle. We heard things like "hang in there," or "we're praying for you," but our family struggled and received no financial help from the church during those four years.

My dad had an old blue Rambler that was given to him, and he drove it around everywhere. Let me tell you this—I was so embarrassed to get into that vehicle. It was so loud that you could hear Dad coming from eight blocks away. When Dad would come and pick me up from basketball practice, the guys riding with us always knew when my dad was coming because of how loud that car was. That old Rambler had a hole in the floor in the back. When it rained we would get wet from the water splashing up from the ground.

That Rambler took us to our religious gatherings every Sunday morning, Sunday evening, and Wednesday evening faithfully. Our church building sat on top of a pretty big hill, so let me tell you if we had ever been late (which we never were) that car would have interrupted the service it was so loud. As a young child riding in that old Rambler with water splashing on us I wondered if anyone at our local church would believe and behave on our behalf as the early church did. I was very appreciative of the camp scholarships that they gave my siblings and me And the youth trips we got to attend, but my dad was in need of some real help.

I came to realize later on in life that church programs and activities are designed like the matrix. They keep us occupied and we feel obligated to them. We feel guilty when we can't fulfill those obligations; then the minister preaches a sermon on being involved in the life of the church and half the church comes forward to repent with bitter tears and feelings of shame. We have to be cautious about crossing the line between leading people to be compelled by the love of Christ and mind control and manipulation. When people are manipulated by sermons from preachers using bad theology, people feel condemned and you can get them to make an emotional decision. They will give more, do more, try harder to win God's approval. It is not a true heart conversion and you can lead them just about anywhere you want them to go.

My dad was too proud to get on welfare and government assistance, but there was a different kind of government program I believe he was searching for. "For to us a child is born, to us a son is given, and the government will be on his shoulders. And he will be called Wonderful Counselor, Mighty God, Everlasting Father, Prince of Peace. Of the increase of his government and peace there will be no end." (Isaiah 9:6-7.) I believe this is the type of government help my family needed when my dad was without a job for four years. You see, Jesus came to bring a government, not a religion or a denomination.

In Acts 2, we see his government at work among the citizens of his kingdom. Those who had gave to those who didn't have in order that everybody could have. This is what is known as *commonwealth* which is practiced in kingdoms. This is the kingdom that Jesus came to give us and he admonished us to repent or change our minds because this kingdom or this government has arrived.

Whatever a person believes is usually reflected by how a person behaves. The problem with growing up in a denomination is behavior takes precedent over belief. If you don't know what you believe or why you believe it, then how can you behave according to that belief system? When Thomas touched Jesus' hands and side he would never have to question his belief system again. When you grow up in religion yet never have an encounter with the risen Savior, then your behavior will be a reflection of your belief. When your belief system is based upon Bible camps, youth rallies, VBS, and religious gatherings, then your behavior will focus on keeping a good public image. Then Jesus cried out, "When a man believes in me, he does not believe in me only, but in the one who sent me. I have come into the world as a light, so that no one who believes in me should stay in darkness"(John 12:44-45.)

Denominations have done the opposite of what Jesus describes in John 12. They have kept people in darkness and away from the light that has come into the world. I was more loyal to my denomination and its doctrinal teachings than I was to Jesus and his kingdom. My belief system was formed from the time I was a child to believe we were the only group that interpreted the Bible correctly and behaved the way the Bible told us to behave. I believed that if you were not part of my denomination then you had stamped your ticket for a one-way trip to the hell fire prepared for Satan and his angels. My belief system is one of the reasons why I experimented in college with things that were ungodly and unrighteous. Religious activities left me empty when what I desired was an encounter with the risen Savior.

Jesus mentions that belief in him would keep us out of the darkness. Another word for darkness is *ignorance*. This word implies lack of knowledge. You can have multiple degrees from a religious institution and still be ignorant. It is possible to graduate with honors from a religious school of higher learning and still be in darkness. Religion keeps people in darkness, but belief in Jesus exposes us to the light. Some religious institutions train potential ministers, pastors, teachers, and missionaries in darkness. I know this is a strong statement, but I am a living witness to this fact. I received my undergraduate degree from a Christian institution where every semester we were required to take a Bible or religious course. In five years (it took me a little longer) I did not have one course on the kingdom. I was taught different subjects by professors who believed the doctrinal creeds of our particular denomination, so in a sense I was learning more about how they interpreted what God said than what God really said. I then received a Master's degree from another religious institution affiliated with my denomination. I must admit they were much more opened to the Holy Spirit and the study of scripture than my experience in undergrad.

Jesus says that we are to seek after the kingdom and his righteousness first (Matthew 6:33.) Seeking implies that we pursue or go after it. The kingdom is the object of this pursuit, and *first* means it is priority. How can a minister in training go through almost eight years of educational training and never have a class on what Jesus says is priority? Some of the things I studied included Old and New Testament history, Christian ethics, marriage and family, doctrine classes, mission classes, Paul's letters, etc., but not one class on the kingdom.

"For he has rescued us from the dominion of darkness and brought us into the kingdom of the Son he loves". (Colossians 1:13.) We have been rescued from ignorance into the kingdom of light. I'm afraid that religion is still handing out degrees in darkness. Remember earlier I mentioned growing up listening to black preachers in my denomination and before they got up to speak the person introducing them would go through their list of degrees and accomplishments? Well, how could someone with that much education get in front of hundreds of people and declare if someone uses an instrument they are going to hell, or if they don't have the right name on their sign in front of the building they are going to hell. These are things I heard as a kid growing up and they helped shape my belief system. Remember what Jesus said about belief? When a man believes in me, he does not believe in me only, but in the one who sent me. This statement has nothing to do with religious beliefs that some denomination made up, but simply implies belief in Jesus!

Now some may believe I'm throwing my denomination under the bus from my personal experience. I'm not a disgruntled former member of a particular denomination. My concern is people are not able to encounter the risen Christ by faith because organized religion has hidden him behind the impenetrable cloud called religion.

I can't believe that Jesus intended his kingdom to be Baptist, Catholic, Protestant, Pentecostal, Lutheran, Conservative, Liberal, instrumental or non-instrumental, and the list can go on forever. Each denomination has its own schools with its own doctrinal teachings, and its own hand-picked professors. Some schools won't allow a professor to teach at their institution if they are not affiliated with the school's particular denomination. Is this what Jesus intended? This is how the impenetrable cloud of religion became the veil that hid God from my sight.

Chapter Six

RELIGION WAS NOT DESIGNED TO FULFILL PEOPLE.

I n John 3 when Nicodemus came to visit Jesus at night, it was like a game of "hide and seek." Nicodemus was a Pharisee and a member of the ruling council which means he was an educated man. But like many of our teachers and preachers today, Nicodemus was educated but still in darkness. After hearing and seeing Jesus, Nicodemus realized that there was something different about Jesus. Nicodemus said, "Rabbi, we know you are a teacher who has come from God. For no one could perform the miraculous signs you are doing if God were not with him" (John 3:2.)

What is it that Nicodemus was seeking after? He had a position of authority, power, and was well respected by many. So why is he coming to Jesus seeking? Could there be something else Nicodemus was searching for that couldn't be found in his religious rituals, or the pages of all the books and manuscripts he read and studied? Nicodemus was seeking after what everyone in religion today is seeking after, the kingdom! Jesus' miracles were evidence to people that the kingdom had come back to earth again (See Luke 11:20.) People were in awe of the miraculous signs that Jesus performed, and Nicodemus was aware enough to know that God was with Jesus because of these signs. It is interesting that Nicodemus did not go to the local religious library to find what he was looking for. He did not seek the advice of other members from the ruling council. Jesus knew exactly what Nicodemus was looking for. He was looking for something that a religious experience as a Pharisee couldn't give him—Not a ceremonial washing, the avoidance from a leper, attendance at a synagogue meeting, or his title or position. Before he could even tell Jesus why he came to him in the middle of the night, Jesus replied, "I tell you the truth, no one can see the kingdom of God unless he is born again" (John 3:3.) "Here it is," Jesus told Nicodemus. "You are coming to me looking for the kingdom because that is what man lost in the garden. All of your religious attempts to experience the kingdom again have failed." Nicodemus could not find the kingdom in all the rules and ceremonies that the Pharisees kept. Even though the Old Testament scriptures which he was an expert in testified to this kingdom, it was hidden from Nicodemus by religion.

As Jesus begins to explain to Nicodemus how to get into the kingdom, Nicodemus replies, "How can this be?" This question that Nicodemus asked is still being asked today. "How can this be?" We have tried to get the kingdom by changing the music in worship from traditional to contemporary, by putting the most charismatic man in the pulpit to draw in the crowds. We've created programs that will attract young people with families, started new ministries, and promoted churches that are seeker friendly. We've advertised to people by telling them they don't have to dress up to come to church. They can have a latte and a doughnut while the service is going on. Organized religion has pulled out all of the gimmicks in order to answer the same question that Nicodemus asked Jesus, "How can this be?"

As Jesus traveled through the towns and villages preaching the good news about the kingdom, he saw something that most of us—if we would open our eyes—would see. "When he saw the crowds, he had compassion on them, because they were harassed and helpless, like sheep without a shepherd". (Matthew 9:36.) If our spiritual eyes were open to the harvest, we would see the same thing Jesus saw. People hurting, helpless, and harassed. We can live our lives and only see what we want to see. If we don't want to see the condition that most inner city public school systems are in, we don't have to. If we don't want to see the issues of hunger right in our own backyards, then we don't have to. If we don't want to see the crime, violence, dropout rates, unemployment rates, drug abuse, sexual abuse, and all the issues that plague our major cities, then we don't have to. We can buy our dream home 30 minutes away from all of those things, put up our ten-foot privacy fence, and pretend none of those things are happening around us. We can do all of this while we still go to church services every Sunday and get involved in the life of our local church and earn membership reward points.

The sad truth is that most of the harassment that helpless and hurting people endure comes from religious people offering people empty promises of a religious experience through a seminar, a Bring Your Friend Day at church, a conference, or some type of religious meeting.

This is a true story, so listen closely. A family was in need of financial assistance and went to their local church leadership. This was the same local church that this particular family would put money in the offering basket every Sunday. This request for financial assistance was a onetime request to be paid back to the church. The leadership put their heads together and told the family they couldn't help them because if they did they would be obligated to help everyone who comes to them and ask for financial help. This is what religion offers people? You are told that you are to tithe every Sunday so the church can remain operational, but if you ever need help from the money that you have been putting in the basket then there has to be a meeting. They must see if you qualify or are eligible to receive the funds. "Give to the one who asks you, and do not turn away from the one who wants to borrow from you". (Matthew 5:42.)

Can we please just be honest and let the people know where their money is going every Sunday? It is going to pay for the multi-million dollar facility that holds the corporate worship assembly. It is going to pay for all the bells and whistles needed to keep people's attention while they sit in the multi-million dollar building. It is going to pay the salaries of the staff that operates the religious programs and leads the flock. It is going to pay to heat and cool the multi-million dollar facility. It is going to the upkeep of the multi-million dollar facility when things like the AC unit break down or a new roof or parking lot is needed.

Please stop saying we are giving this money to the Lord, because I have never seen someone write a check that says "pay to the order of God." We don't need to use mind-control and manipulation to get people to give. Just tell them the truth and they probably will give anyway, we don't have to preach sermons about giving to make people feel bad and run to the altar to repent for keeping God's money. I'm not mentioning these things and calling them wrong or evil, but let's just be honest and tell people what we are doing with the money. When the people who give the money have a need, let's meet those needs.

Now back to Jesus. Right after his statement in Matthew 9:36, Jesus calls his disciples together and gives them authority to drive out evil spirits and heal every sickness and disease. Remember the miracles are evidence that the kingdom has come back to earth, so Jesus gave his disciples power to exercise their kingdom authority. Remember right before this Jesus saw the hurting and helpless people and had compassion on them. What do harassed and helpless people really need? Do they need a church service to attend, a program to be a part of, or a denomination to become a member of? What is it they really need? Jesus answers this question "As you go, preach this message: "The kingdom of heaven is near." (Matthew 10:7.)

You got it, what people are seeking after is the kingdom! Jesus tells his disciples specifically what message to preach as they go out among the helpless, harassed, and hurting people. Take the kingdom message to the people and show people that the kingdom is back on earth to heal the sick, raise the dead, cleanse those who have leprosy, drive out demons.

A question that religious denominations have to ask themselves is *"What message are we preaching? What message are we training our future missionaries, pastors, teachers, and preachers to spread to hurting people? Are we simply teaching them the doctrinal teachings of our particular denomination or are we teaching them the message that Jesus taught his disciples?* Again, Jesus says, "As you go, preach this message." This is a very specific command. He did not want the disciples preaching any other messages beside the kingdom.

After almost nine years of preaching in Cincinnati, I came before our assembly and confessed to them that I had been preaching messages about Jesus, but not preaching the message that Jesus preached. I went through a period of confession and repentance for not preaching the message of the kingdom all these years. I had seminary training and thought I was doing a good job preaching the Word, but I had been trained in darkness. I was trained to preach good messages, but not the good news. I was like Nicodemus, I had the degree and the accomplishments, but I was still searching for something. So, even after a B.S in Psychology, a M.A in Missiology, and eight and a half years of public preaching, I was still playing hide and seek.

Chapter Seven

WHAT DENOMINATIONS DON'T WANT YOU TO KNOW

B est selling author and Pastor of Bahamas Faith Ministries Myles Munroe stated in an interview that "the result of religion is exclusivism, separatism, racism, and terrorism". This is a pretty heavy statement, I know, but allow me a few pages to explain.

Let's define two words before we continue. First, what is religion? Religions are simply attempts from man to connect with God, some form of a higher power, or the universe. Man creates rituals, customs, and traditions, and abides by written and unwritten codes to follow in order to align themselves with the god they are attempting to worship. Secondly, the word *denomination* implies one applicable to each individual of a class; distinctively named church or sect. If you put the two words together you have religious denomination, and that is how I have referenced the particular group I grew up in.

There are reportedly 38,000 different Christian denominations from Catholics to Protestants, Latter Day Saints, Nontrinitarian, Messianic Judaism, Jewish Christian, New Thought, Esoteric Christian, and the list can go on for pages. In the name of religion, more blood has been shed and more lives have been lost than any of the World Wars.

One of the darkest days in US history took place September 11, 2001, when in the name of religion the World Trade Center towers came down, claiming the lives of thousands of people. I will never forget the images of the planes crashing into the towers and exploding immediately on impact, the images of people jumping to their deaths, and the image of the towers tumbling to the ground. What kind of religion would lead to the death of thousands of people? Well, before we condemn everyone in Middle Eastern countries claiming Islam as their religion, let's not so quickly forget our western religious history. Europeans came to this country in the name of religious freedom and political freedom and killed off Indians who were already settled here. They enslaved Africans during slave trading and the southern colonies grew economically because of free labor. If the purpose of coming to the new world was religious freedom, then why were tribes of Indians thrown off their land and Africans brought over here as slaves?

I grew up being taught that my denomination was the restored New Testament church, and that we were the only group who practiced this restored form of a pure biblical religion. I grew up being taught that if you were not part of my particular denomination and did not practice religion the way we did then you were condemned to hell. Can you imagine teaching a young child that all of his friends who go to church like I did every Sunday, live the same moral life day to day, and love Jesus the same way would burn in hell because they did not practice religion the way I did, or worship God exactly the way I worshiped? In the history of this country and in the name of religiosity, tribes of Indians were thrown off their land and a nation of Africans were enslaved, mistreated, separated from their families, and deprived of rights as citizens in a nation that was governed by religion.

In Genesis 1:26 God's mandate for his creation is for mankind to exercise dominion over the earth not each other. Listen to this description of God's kingdom: "Righteousness and justice are the foundation of your throne; love and faithfulness go before you." (Psalm 89:14.)

Religious people are some of the most dangerous people on earth. Listen to the way the Apostle Paul describes his former life as a religious Pharisee: "For you have heard of my previous way of life in Judaism, how intensely I persecuted the church of God and tried to destroy it" (Galatians 1:13.) Before Paul encountered the risen Savior, his life was wrapped up in religion. "I was advancing in Judaism beyond many Jews of my own age and was extremely zealous for the traditions of my fathers" (Galatians 1:14.) In his zeal for Judaism he tried to destroy the church of the Lord. In my zeal for the denomination I was associated with, everyone was going to hell who was not part of it. Religion will keep you in the dark and make you believe what you are doing is for God. Just as in Paul's day people were persecuted and killed in the name of religion and that trend has not stopped centuries later. Whether it's Paul persecuting people, or nations oppressing other nations, or people flying planes into buildings, religious people are dangerous.

My mindset was far from flying planes into buildings or strapping a bomb around a person to go into a crowded place to destroy the lives of innocent people, but in principle it is not that far off. Instead of being strapped with a bomb, I was strapped with verses of scriptures ready to blow up anyone who didn't believe or worship the way I did. The greatest problem in the world today is not the economic recession, the war on terror, or gas prices. It is religion.

My religious experience is a clear example of how religion produces exclusivism. This theology shaped my thinking into believing that I was elite and above anyone else who was part of another denomination other than mine. Does this remind you of anybody in the New Testament? "Woe to you, teachers of the law and Pharisees, you hypocrites! You shut the kingdom of heaven in men's faces. You yourselves do not enter, nor will you let those enter who are trying" (Matthew 23:13.) Because of this elitist attitude, my theology was being formed and I was shutting the kingdom of heaven in men's faces.

My denomination would not allow anyone who was not part of our particular school of thought to participate or fellowship with us in anything. This is the reason why I say one of the results of religion is exclusivism. My denomination excluded all those who did not share the same name and theological convictions that we did. Even as a kid I always wondered deep down how we could be the only group of the more than 38,000 different denominations to be right. In a sense, I would wonder if 37,999 different groups could be entirely wrong and my particular denomination be the only one that has it all right. Well, by mind control and manipulation, I believed, growing up, that all of my friends were doomed to hell because they didn't practice religion the way I did.

Another result of religion is separatism and by this I mean my denomination separated itself from all other denominations by claiming we were non-denominational and separate from any other religious organization because we were the only church found in the New Testament. As mentioned earlier in chapter 4, we prided ourselves in restoring the church of the first century Christians.

One of the scriptures my denomination used to support the church being the only one in the New Testament was "Greet one another with a holy kiss. All the churches of Christ send greetings" (Romans 16:16.) Now, I saw people practicing kissing but I'm not sure it was a holy kiss. They would claim the holy kiss was simply culture, but the second part of this text was used to claim my denomination as the only church found in the Bible. Some of the religious creeds and doctrines that we believed were revelations from God's holy word separated us from any denominational group who practiced any other form of religion. Because we did not use mechanical instruments in corporate worship, we separated ourselves from other groups who did. We took communion every Sunday, not just once a month, so this separated us from all other groups.

We also did not call our minister "reverend" because we believed that only God should be addressed as reverend. Although in the scripture it says God is holy and tells us to be holy as He is holy. So we can be holy as God is, but don't dare call another man "reverend." Now I know we don't walk around addressing each other as holy, but these are issues that we used to separate ourselves from other denominations. Not only did I grow up seeing this exclusivism and separatism in my religious denomination, but these are also issues that the early Christians dealt with because some were still stuck in religion.

The whole chapter of Acts 15 deals with the council at Jerusalem and their attempt to rid the kingdom of God from religious systems that created exclusivism, separatism, and racism. The issue is addressed as follows. "Some men came down from Judea to Antioch and were teaching the brothers: 'Unless you are circumcised, according to the custom of Moses, you cannot be saved.'" (Acts 15:1.) These brothers teaching this turned physical circumcision into a salvation issue. Thank goodness for Paul and Barnabas who understood the kingdom of God and would not stand for religion. They sharply debated these brothers over this issue. Now this issue sounds very similar to religions today who make claims like "if you don't worship the way we worship you can't be saved, if you don't do what we do in our religious meetings you can't be saved." Anytime you attempt to elevate religious practices over the kingdom the result will be exclusivism, separatism, or racism.

In Galatians chapter 2 Paul who debated the brothers over the issue of circumcision at the Jerusalem council had to oppose Peter because Peter reverted back to religion instead of living in the kingdom. "Before certain men came from James, he used to eat with the Gentiles. But when they arrived, he began to draw back and separate himself from the Gentiles because he was afraid of those who belonged to the circumcision group". (Galatians 2:12.) There are a few key phrases in this verse we need to give some attention to.

The first is he began to *separate*. As we are discussing in this chapter, practicing religion separates people into groups although claiming to be one they have a particular distinction. Another key concept regarding Peter is *he was afraid*. Religion also encourages us to operate in fear. Peter was guilty of operating out of fear of how the Jews would perceive him if seen eating with uncircumcised believers. This is another result of religion; it keeps us in fear. "For God did not give us a spirit of timidity, but a spirit of power, of love and of self-discipline" (II Timothy 1:7.) A spirit of timidity or fear does not come from God, but it is used for manipulation to control the actions of people.

Not only does religion use fear as a tactic of manipulation, but governments also use it to control the actions of people. In a Gallup Poll dated September 2, 2011, a poll was taken asking Americans how safe they felt that the government could protect its citizens from another terrorists attack on US soil. The poll showed that since the capture of Osama bin Laden fear of an attack has retreated from the high level, and it is now on the low end of the range seen over the past decade. When the government puts a terror alert out it is represented by a color code. Red is severe, orange is high, yellow is elevated, blue is guarded, and green is low. A red or orange alert will take a whole nation into panic. People will begin stock-piling water bottles, bags of rice, and non-perishables , and stocking their basements taking refuge in bunkers. I'm only using this example to show that if people are in fear, their actions can be controlled. The same principle goes for religion. If people are in fear, then it is easier to control the actions of the people.

We were taught if we were not members of our particular denomination and if we did not practice religion a certain way, we were doomed to hell. This is a fear tactic used to control and manipulate the actions of followers.

We were told God would punish us eternally if we did not conform to the pattern of this restored New Testament way of church. We were told and convinced that this was the only way that God would accept our worship, be pleased with our lifestyle, and approve us as his true children—if we followed all the ways, decrees, and doctrines of our denomination. If my religion had a color coded system like the US terror alert, I would have spent most of my life on red (severe). I remember some nights going to bed and fearing going to hell because I had not lived up to the calling of my denomination.

Just as with the Jerusalem council, those who were practicing religion would use the Old Testament scriptures to put fear into those they were trying to get to follow them. Ministers, pastors, and teachers have become experts at manipulating the scriptures (especially to those who don't know them well) and instilling fear in the listeners to get them to do what they want. That is why you see the most charismatic, dynamic, and extraverted guys in the pulpit today because it's all about the presentation. In religion it's not really about the substance, but how the substance is presented.

The apostle Paul understood it was all about the substance and not the presentation. He declares that the power of God for the salvation of man is in the gospel(Romans 1:16.) Paul also understood it was not about the presentation. He says, "When I came to you, brothers and sisters I did not come with eloquence or superior wisdom as I proclaimed to you the testimony about God" (I Corinthians 2:1.) If it is presented in a way that will move people emotionally to a decision, then you can convince thousands of people to do anything you want.

This leads to our next discussion and that is the next result of religion is *racism*. Martin Luther King, Jr. made a comment many years ago: "The most segregated day in America is Sunday morning." As seen through the biblical references we just visited in Acts and Galatians, racism has been a result of religion for thousands of years. Circumcised groups despised uncircumcised groups, Jews despised Gentiles, Jews despised Samaritans, Jews despised the Romans, etc. In this modern day religious world how much of that has really changed? Now, I would be totally off base to say that we have not made progress in this area, but as long as we pursue religion instead of the kingdom this issue of racism will ever be before us.

In my denomination, the local church that I grew up in was racially diverse, and we were the only local church in the city that could make that claim at the time. My denomination has a history dealing with racism due to the fact the movement has its roots in the southern states in the Bible Belt. Other books have been written by authors such as Richard T. Hughes, C. Leonard Allen, and Edwin J. Robinson, to name a few, to deal with the history and the issue of race in my denomination, but I want to simply deal with a few facts for the purpose of this writing.

The first issue I want to challenge is the labeling of denominations as Black churches and White churches. You hear people ask, "Is it a White church or Black church?" as they inquire about it before visiting or attending. The first thing everyone needs to know that religion won't tell us is it is not Black or White it is Jesus'. Religious denominations reflect an earthly culture (e,g., Black, White, Hispanic, Asian, etc.) while kingdom churches reflect a heavenly culture. Religious people play the blame game about who started racism and who is to blame for racism in the body of Christ, but kingdom citizens look for resolutions through the Spirit and attempt to make the body of Christ reflect our heavenly culture.

I totally understand that because of this fallen world we live in and how powerful religious denominations have become there are always going to be people separating themselves into racial, socio-economic, and geographical groups, but it should be the goal of every kingdom citizen to reflect the culture of heaven instead of this earthly culture. We are here on earth, but we are not from here. Paul says, "But our citizenship is in heaven" (Philippians 3:20.) This is a powerful statement from Paul concerning kingdom heritage in the body of Christ. How can I be racist against a citizen that is from the exact same place I am? How can a citizen of heaven hold a racist attitude against another citizen of heaven?

The first question we have to answer is "Where are we from?" A citizen is an inhabitant of a city, a townsman, a member of a state. Since our citizenship is in heaven, we are all members from the same place. The reason why racism is one result of religion is because all religions have their origin here on earth. They were created by man who is a fallen being. Religions are simply attempts for man to connect with God, some form of a higher power, or the universe. Man creates rituals, customs, and traditions, and abides by written and unwritten codes to follow in order to align themselves with the god they are attempting to worship.

My denomination is no different and we have a dark past when it comes to racism. I'm not bringing up these facts to open old wounds, but simply to make a point that when you operate in a denomination the results will not be kingdom. The reason we look at the story in Acts 15 of the Jerusalem council, and Paul opposing Peter is not to make Peter look bad and accuse him of being racist, but to learn so history will not repeat itself.

Several of our institutes of higher learning during the dark racist days of the 60's caved in to the social culture instead of believing God and allowing the kingdom culture to prevail. In several of the southern schools in my denomination Blacks were not allowed to attend because of the pressure of the southern Jim Crow laws. Now remember, my denomination claimed they were the restored church of the 1st century New Testament and the only ones qualified to make it to heaven. How can you make a claim to be headed to a place (heaven) where there is no racism, but yet no blacks are allowed to study at your institution. Again, I want to emphasize that things have changed and those schools are integrated. I actually studied at one of them but my point is when we deal with religion the result is always exclusivism, separatism, racism, and terrorism. Now even today a lot of churches in my denomination as well as others are predominately White or Black churches, so I ask do we reflect the kingdom of heaven or do we reflect an earthly man made religion?

Chapter Eight

THE SPIRIT—
THE GREAT EQUALIZER

In the history of man we have witnessed many different movements led by great leaders in an attempt to bring equality, whether social, political, racial, or gender, to all. A few have been The American Indian movement, Civil rights movement, human rights movement, right to life movement, Apartheid in South Africa, and the women's liberation movement. Since sin was introduced to the world. in the Garden of Eden, inequality, social injustice, and segregation of all sorts have plagued every civilization.

The first act recorded after being expelled from the garden was a brother (Cain) taking the life of another brother (Abel) because of jealousy over a sacrifice. After Cain murdered his brother, the Bible says he left the Lord's presence and lived in the land of Nod. Then Cain had a son, named him Enoch, and started building a city he named after his son. Man to this point has gone from a place that God planted and placed his creation where His presence was always there (Eden) to Cain leaving the presence of the Lord and building a city (Enoch). Man has built cities, civilizations, created cultures, established military forces, and built dynasties to dominate one another at the expense of other human beings. By the time we get to Genesis 6, The Lord sees how great man's wickedness has become on the earth, and how every inclination of the thoughts of his heart was evil all the time (Genesis 6:5.)

When Adam rebelled against God in the garden, it left man without the presence of God in the form of the Holy Spirit. Man was left to navigate through the world he lived in using his five senses and whatever he thought was right. So if man wanted to treat woman as if she were property and a secondhand citizen, then man did what he thought was right. If man wanted to elevate the birth of a son over the birth of a daughter and treat the son as a prize possession and the daughter as something less or undesirable, then he did what he thought was right. If one race decided they were far more superior than another race for whatever reason, then the culture was created and people acted according to their beliefs. If one religion believed they were better than another religion the belief system was established, and the people acted accordingly to what they believed. This is how we got to where we are today. Movements have to be established, wars have to occur, and protests have to ring out in the streets in order for social equality, justice, and righteousness to manifest itself in the societies that have been created by man.

Are we in need of another political, civil, or religious movement? Are we in need of another protest? Do we need another Nelson Mandela, Martin Luther King, Jr., Mother Teresa, Ghandi, Fred Shuttlesworth, or Harriet Tubman to arise and fight for equality? All of the movements we have witnessed in the past and even those still seen today are worthy and noble. The men and women whose courage and faith help lead these movements will always be remembered and their impact and influence will always be with us. But there is one movement that is the great equalizer to all of the movements, protests, marches, wars, and even great leaders that our history has witnessed. We are not in need of another political or social movement, a civil rights movement, or a liberation movement. What we are looking for is something that can't be found in the streets and lines of a demonstration, a march on Washington, a protest in front of a corporate building, or picket signs in front of an abortion clinic. What we are looking for is what we as humans lost when Adam rebelled in the Garden of Eden. We are looking for the Holy Spirit, the great equalizer!

The prophet Joel speaks of a new era and time that was to come, and what this new era would usher into the hearts of mankind again. Joel prophesies,"And afterward, I will pour out my Spirit on all people. Your sons and daughters will prophesy, your old men will dream dreams, your young men will see visions. Even on my servants, both men and women, I will pour out my Spirit in those days" (Joel 2:28-29.) This prophesy mentions the time when the Holy Spirit, the great equalizer, would be poured out back into the lives of God's people again. A day was on the horizon when God once again would allow his Holy Spirit to indwell his prized possession—mankind. Up to this point the Holy Spirit could not indwell man again because of his rebellion. "Then the Lord said, 'My Spirit will not contend with man forever, for he is mortal; his days will be a hundred and twenty years' (Genesis 6:3.) God's Spirit could not live in man because of man's sin and rebellion, but God made a promise and through the prophet Joel gave hope that once again there would be an outpouring of His Spirit on man.

The move that man has been waiting for and searching for God has already provided. When Peter preached on Pentecost, he quoted Joel's prophecy because the time had come for the Spirit to be poured out on mankind again. The Spirit helps us to connect with God, relate to God, and function like God.It gives us the mind of Christ (I Corinthians 2:16). If the Spirit, the great equalizer, is leading a person's life then there is a production going on initiated by the Spirit in the life of the individual who is yielded to the working of the Spirit. Here is the result of a life yielded to the Spirit: love, joy, peace, patience, kindness, goodness, faithfulness, gentleness, and self-control. This is what is known as the fruit of the Spirit, and if these characteristics are present in the life of a civilization, a culture, a city, leadership, a government, or a country, how could there ever be racism, terrorism, separatism, segregation, social inequality, hunger, and all the things that plague our world and keep people in bondage? "Blessed is the nation whose God is the Lord, the people he chose for his inheritance" (Psalm 33:12.) Our Declaration of Independence claims that every citizen has the right to life, liberty, and the pursuit of happiness. We as kingdom citizens know that Jesus came that we may have life and have it more abundantly (John 10:10), and liberty is found where the Spirit is (II Corinthians 3:17.) So maybe instead of chasing the American Dream we should be in pursuit of God who offers us salvation through Jesus, by the Holy Spirit.

The question is: *are we under the influence, guidance, and yielding of the Holy Spirit?* This goes far beyond following religious rituals, creeds, and rules. It goes far beyond associating ourselves with a particular denomination, finding a church that meets all our needs when we want and how we want. There is absolutely no way a person can be under the influence of the Holy Spirit and be racist toward another person, believe they are superior to another, segregate themselves from other people, believe one gender is superior to another.

In Joel's prophecy, he puts an end to the social structures that man created, gender roles that separate people, socio-economic walls that have been put up, and even age discrimination. When Christ released the Spirit after his death, the movement began so that we didn't have to divide ourselves over these issues any longer. Paul says because of this promised Holy Spirit that indwells man we are all sons of God (Galatians 4:7.) Paul clearly states there is neither Jew nor Greek (racial boundaries), slave nor free (social boundaries), male nor female (gender boundaries), for you all are one in Christ Jesus (Galatians 3:28.)

The world is not in need of another social, political, or civil movement, but it is in need of a movement of the Holy Spirit, the great equalizer. Belief in Jesus and the promised Holy Spirit brings liberation to all, freedom to all, life to all. It does not separate people into categories, it does not separate races of people, it does not exclude certain denominations who believe certain things. The Spirit, the great equalizer, unites all those to the Father through belief in Jesus Christ, and we are all part of one body.

For too long we have practiced religion and been led by denominational creeds and rules instead of being led by the Spirit of God. We have devoted ourselves and our lives and pledged allegiance to a manmade denomination instead of the Spirit of God. The result of that is evident by all the different religious denominations represented in the world today. The power of God, revealed through his Son Jesus who released the Holy Spirit, has been hidden from us by this impenetrable cloud of religion. Instead of seeing the fruit of the Spirit in our world today, we have partaken of the forbidden fruit again and have hid ourselves from the presence of God who is seeking us and looking for some accountability.. We have occupied our lives and all of our time seeking after religious activities and making sure we are performing those activities correctly instead of allowing the Spirit to work in our lives to bring about the fruit that only He can produce.

I believe that God is tired of our religious efforts and our search for him through meaningless activities. God warns the church in Sardis: "These are the words of him who holds the seven spirits of God and the seven stars. I know your deeds; you have a reputation of being alive, but you are dead" (Revelation 3:1.)

Another prophet of God in the Old Testament delivered a message to the children of Israel concerning their futile religious activities without righteousness, justice, and mercy. Listen to what the prophet Amos says concerning Israel's religious activities. "I hate, I despise your religious feasts; I cannot stand your assemblies. Even though you bring me burnt offerings and grain offerings, I will not accept them. Though you bring choice fellowship offerings I will have no regard for them. Away with the noise of your songs! I will not listen to the music of your harps. But let justice roll on like a river, righteousness like a never-failing stream!" (Amos 5:21-24.) God is more interested in his kingdom coming to earth and influencing and impacting the lives of his creation than he is our religious activity.

How many assemblies does God reject every Sunday or whatever day people gather today on around the world? Can God be pleased with an assembly of people who are worshipping together who think they are the only group of people of the 6.9 billion people on earth going to heaven? Can he be pleased with a group of people who come together every Sunday to participate in rituals and activities and think of all the people on earth they are the only ones worshipping him the proper way? Can God be pleased with an assembly of people whose building is right next to a community that is broken and filled with poverty while those assembled sit on cushion seats, drink coffee, and eat doughnuts, but won't welcome the residents of that community to fellowship with them because they are different?

Again, God's concern and his priority is that his kingdom impact this earth through those he has put his Holy Spirit in. We can no longer use our places of worship as Adam and Eve used the trees in the garden to hide from the presence of God. God desires and wants more than just our assemblies .He wants our Holy Spirit- led lives to impact and influence this world we live in. I believe God is in heaven with his fingers in his ears on most Sundays because we have fallen into the same trap that the nation of Israel fell into when Amos prophesied to them. So much energy, effort, resources, and time goes into our assemblies while injustice, inequality, and unrighteousness goes on around us. God gave us his Spirit so we could reflect his nature and take that nature outside of the building walls and start impacting this world for him. We have settled for religion and religious activities in place of real kingdom living. We are hiding from the presence of God, and religion has put a veil over our eyes so we can't see what God truly intended for the people to whom he gave his Holy Spirit.

When a person lives by the Holy Spirit, the desires of the sinful nature are not gratified (Galatians 5:16.) Living by the Spirit transforms the moral compass in society. Those who chose to live this Spirit-led life will put to death the acts of the sinful nature and live a life producing the fruit of the Spirit. Paul discusses the difference between a life led by the Spirit and a life led by the sinful nature. "Those who live according to the sinful nature have their minds set on what that nature desires; but those who live in accordance with the Spirit have their minds set on what the Spirit desires (Romans 8:5.)

Can a person led by the Spirit be racist? Can a person led by the Spirit be a terrorist? Can a person led by the Spirit kill others for not believing in their religious convictions? Can a person led by the Spirit not allow a certain ethnic group to attend their college? The answer to each of these questions is obviously no. A person not being led by the Spirit of God is capable of doing any and everything. "The acts of the sinful nature are obvious: sexual immorality, impurity, and debauchery; jealousy, fits of rage, selfish ambition, dissensions, factions and envy; drunkenness, orgies, and the like" (Galatians 5:22-23.) As believers we don't live under the influence of the sinful nature. "Those who belong to Christ Jesus have crucified the sinful nature with its passions and desires" (Galatians 5:24.) You can be religious and still produce the fruit of the sinful nature as mentioned earlier with Paul's former life in Judaism. You can be religious and still be racist as we saw with Peter's interaction with the Gentile believers. He chose to operate in the flesh at that moment instead of being led by the Spirit. "Those who are in the realm of the flesh cannot please God". (Romans 8:8.) No matter how hard we try or no matter how many religious activities we involve ourselves in, if we are not led by the Spirit God is not pleased.

FINAL REFLECTIONS

I recently had a phone conversation with my mom and we were talking about how man-made religion influences the lives of so many people in a negative way. My mom growing up was part of a denomination who believed they were the only true restored New Testament church. When my mom met my dad he was part of another denomination. So my mom was in a pretty tough situation. The man she was falling in love with was not a part of her religious group and she was forbidden to marry outside of her religious group. Anyone of a different belief was considered a nonbeliever. Because of religion, the local preacher from my mom's denomination refused to marry my parents in their building because they believed her marrying my dad would bring disgrace to their religious belief system.

By God's grace, my mom and dad's love for one another was stronger than the religious obstacles that were put in their way. They ended up having the wedding ceremony on my great-grandmother's front porch. My parents stayed married for nearly 40 years until my dad passed away eight years ago from a cancerous brain tumor. I began to reflect on my mom and dad's marriage; they were fruitful and multiplied, bringing six kids into the world. They both loved the Lord and loved each other and gave us a great example of what a kingdom marriage is suppose to look like.

If my parents had allowed religion to have its way and had not united in marriage, then I would not be writing this book right now. If they had caved in to the pressure religion burdens people with, I would not have an 18+-year marriage with my beautiful wife Carla. We would not have been able to be fruitful and multiply, bringing in Jalin Elisha, Dominic Isaiah, and James Edward Pugh III. If religion had had its way, my call to ministry and my dream to plant a church in Cincinnati, Ohio, in the inner city would have never been realized. The thousands of lives that our ministry has impacted for Christ the last 12 years would have never been realized. I reflect, on all the people whom my dad took in our home to live with us while they were going through difficult times. That would never have happened if religion had had its way with my parents.

When we laid my dad to his final rest September 2005, we didn't have a funeral for him. As a matter of fact, Dad didn't even want us to have a viewing. Dad would always tell Mom, "If people want to see me and give me flowers, they need to do it while I'm alive and I can see them." Even with all that we still had a viewing and visitation. I remember that at the funeral home all the way out to the parking lot extended a line of the people who wanted to come and pay respects to my dad and encourage our family. It was like a reunion! The atmosphere was celebratory, just like my dad wanted. He didn't want people crying, screaming, and yelling. He wanted people that knew him to be joyous and appreciative of the time they got to spend with him. Anyone who got the privilege of knowing my dad was blessed beyond measure to be in his presence. He demanded respect as a man of character and integrity; he loved God, loved his family, and simply put was just a good ole country boy from L. A. (L. A. stands for lower Alabama).

I mention my dad because besides God he was and is the greatest influence in my life. I bring up my dad's life to remind myself of how dangerous religion can be. Religion tried to keep my parents from being together, tried to stop a 40-year-marriage from happening and thriving, tried to stop a couple from producing six children who produced 15 grandchildren. Religion tried to keep a couple apart who produced three ministers out of the six kids they had. My oldest brother is a minister outside of St. Louis, my youngest brother is a minister's assistant and worship leader in Dallas, and I am the minister for a church plant in Cincinnati. God has granted me the opportunity to speak in different events and at different churches all across this country.If religion had had its way with my parents, none of this would have been possible.

I want to express how thankful to God I am that he found the real me hiding behind all of my insecurities, my public image, and the religious mask. He searched for me and not only did he find me, but he rescued me from the bondage of religion and set me free to become the person he created. The person he found was someone who was molded and shaped by the denomination he grew up in instead of someone who was created in the image and likeness of God. Now that I'm free, now that I know who I am in Christ Jesus, and now that I'm not bound by religion, streams of living water can freely overflow in my life. Jesus starts out the Sermon on the Mount with this: "Blessed are the poor in spirit: for theirs is the kingdom of heaven" (Matthew 5:3.) Those of us who come to realize that we are spiritually bankrupt, that there are insufficient funds in our spiritual bank accounts, will inherit the kingdom. Realizing that we can do nothing, offer nothing, or even receive nothing apart from God. Ours will be the kingdom. All of my life I believed if I did the activities the way my denomination told me to perform them I was aligned with the kingdom of God. I believed that even if my life didn't line up with my doctrine, if I could just get people to believe I was someone I wasn't then I could still get by. Praise God that I no longer have to hide any more, and the person I am is someone who God is proud to call his son. I'm no longer chasing God only to say Gotcha, but God pursed me, found me, and now I am his son forever

"For the Son of man is come to seek and to save the lost" (Luke 19:10.) Jesus came to deliver to us what we lost in the Garden of Eden. Remember how Adam and Eve hid from the Lord among the trees when God came walking in the cool of day? He came looking for the man he created to rule the earth to find out why they rebelled against his kingdom. God's prized possession of creation hid while God did the seeking. As the story of God and his creation unfolds you read in scripture where God and man are seeking and it becomes a dual seeking. In John 4:23 Jesus says that the Father is seeking after a certain type of worshipper.

In the Old Testament there are several verses that refer to the people of God seeking after Him with their whole beings. "But you will find him if you look for him with all your heart and with all your soul" (Deuteronomy 4:29.) "If my people, who are called by name, will humble themselves and pray and seek my face and turn from their wicked ways, then I will hear from heaven and will forgive their sin and will heal their land" (II Chronicles 7:14.) "Blessed are they who keep his statues and seek him with all their heart" (Psalm 119;2.) "I love those who love me, and those who seek me find me" (Proverbs 8:17.) "You will seek me and find me when you seek me with all your heart" (Jeremiah 29:13.)

In Hebrew, the word for to seek is *baqash* and it means to search out (by any method, specifically in worship or prayer), to strive after, desire, request, or require. The awesome thing about the God we serve is He can never really be caught because He is so beyond us, but if we seek after Him He will allow himself to be found. When the seeker in hide and seek would find everyone, an interchange would take place and the seeker would transition into the hider. God revealed himself to us through the person of Jesus Christ, and when we found Him we found salvation, the forgiveness of sins, and a supernatural empowering of the Holy Spirit. Once we found Him, we chase after Him with all of our might, and we seek first the kingdom and His righteousness. We ask, we knock, we seek, and we find. When God created, it was always his intention to be in intimate relationship with his creation. "They will be my people, and I will be their God" (Jeremiah 32:38) sums up the heart of God for His creation. This has always been God's agenda for His creation, but man in his attempt to seek God (*baqash*) has put up more walls, set up more boundaries, and made it difficult because of religion for people to enter into relationship with God. As you reflect over your life, ask yourself "Am I still seeking after something?" Have you been in church all of your life and you still feel empty? Do you sense there is something more than what you are getting in just your Sunday assemblies? It is a challenge, but if you would empty yourself of you, your religious beliefs, and your preconceived ideas about who you think God is and allow God the creator to find you He will. Through Jesus Christ God will forgive you, cleanse you, and fill you with his Holy Spirit. Will you believe God? No matter where you are hiding or what you are hiding behind, allow God to reveal Himself to you and your life will never be the same.

SCRIPTURE INDEX

ABOUT THE AUTHOR

James Edward Pugh, Jr., was born to James Edward and Barbara Pugh Sr February 5, 1973, in Cincinnati, Ohio. James has been married to his college sweetheart Carla C Pugh for 18 years. They have three children: Jalin Elisha, Dominic Isaiah, and James Edward III. They currently live in Cincinnati, Ohio, where James has served the last 11 years as the minister for Cincinnati Urban Ministry Outreach.

James received his Bachelor's of Science in Psychology from Ohio Valley University in Parkersburg, West Virginiia, in 1996 and received his Master's of Arts from Harding Theological Seminary in Memphis, Tennessee, in 2001.

In 2001, James moved back home to Cincinnati and began work planting a church in the inner city. James travels frequently, speaking at youth events, gospel meetings, and seminars all over the country. Some of James' interests include enjoying his family, watching his boys compete in basketball and football, preaching and teaching about the kingdom of God, and quiet meditation.

James' vision is to proclaim the message of the kingdom through preaching, teaching, and writing. This is the first of many more literary works to come to help proclaim this message of the kingdom that the world needs.

CPSIA information can be obtained at www.ICGtesting.com
Printed in the USA
BVOW03s1201131113

336191BV00003B/587/P